A LETTER GOD MI

Being a poet, being
hur

Rowan Williams

A LETTER GOD MIGHT HAVE WRITTEN

Being a poet, being an archbishop, being human

ISBN 978-1-911221-53-1
2019
Balestier Press
Singapore and London

HEARING OTHERS' VOICES

PA

Contents

1

"Dear Lulu", a letter

Once upon a time there was a child, a little girl. She was called Lulu and she lived in Scotland. She was six years old.

One day Lulu came home from school and she asked her father

'Who invented God?'

Then - she was very sensible - she put it in a letter, 'To God. How did you get invented?'

Trust a child to come up with something like that.

Her dad didn't know, he wasn't really interested in stories about 'God'. But he was a journalist and he was quite sensible too. He sent Lulu's question to several people that he thought might know, like leaders of the great churches around the country.

One of them was me (that was a few years ago when I was Archbishop of Canterbury).

I had never met Lulu, I wish I had, but I thought her question deserved an answer.

I decided that I would try to see what I could do.

So I thought about it a bit - it's my job after all (enjoyable too you know: to think. Hard work at times but I like it. That's why we're here maybe).

Then I sat down and I wrote.

Here is the letter.

'Dear Lulu,

Your dad has sent on your letter and asked if I have any answers. It's a difficult one! But I think God might reply a bit like this –

"Dear Lulu – Nobody invented me – but lots of people discovered me and were quite surprised.

They discovered me when they looked round at the world and thought it was really beautiful or really mysterious and wondered where it came from.

They discovered me when they were very very quiet on their own and felt a sort of peace and love they hadn't expected.

Then they invented ideas about me – some of them sensible and some of them not very sensible.

From time to time I sent them some hints – specially in the life of Jesus – to help them get closer to what I'm really like. But there was nothing and nobody around before me to invent me.

Rather like somebody who writes a story in a book, I started making up the story of the world and eventually invented human beings like you who could ask me awkward questions!"

And then he'd send you lots of love and sign off. I know he doesn't usually write letters, so I have to do the best I can on his behalf.

Lots of love from me too.

+Archbishop Rowan'

Digging deeper

Well, I'd done my best (what more can anyone ask after all?). And actually a lot of people got hold of the letter and really liked it.

One said: 'the best theological statement ever: deep but simple.' She says she keeps it in the back of her Bible to remind her not to get too lost in biblical complications.

Another said:

'Now that's what I call *real* theology! Isn't this exactly why we need theological specialists: not to make the faith more complicated and obscure, but to help us grasp how simple it really is'.

If they're right it is because you I'd been trying to think what would make anything remotely like sense to somebody without any real theological background. Just six years old.

I'd be happy to leave it at that. Simple. But then other, older, people wanted me to say more about it, like what to my mind might lie behind some of these simple thoughts.

Let me try.

I'll take it sentence by sentence.

"Dear Lulu"

Well as I said, I had never met Lulu. But was that any reason why I couldn't try to respond by making contact with her directly and personally (no need for Facebook and all that)? Just as many think God can do. And does. Direct.

"Nobody invented me – but lots of people discovered me and were quite surprised".

The response I wanted to make really was that as with a lot of the most important things in our experience it's discovery rather than Invention that we have to talk about.

One of my great friends, now departed, Donald Nicol, a very impressive writer, used to say that we run our hands down 'the grain of reality' and discovered that it feels rather like what our forebears had felt running their hands down something. Discovering the grain that is already there.

That's what I was saying in my reply. Not starting from what some people think they do. Like 'I'll make up a god!'

I think it is that we find ourselves living in the world in such a way - and perceiving the world in such a way - that something comes through of what I can only call a kind of energy that sustains.

And when you've taken away all the particular ways in which things work and interact, there's *something* that doesn't just *interact*, that simply *acts*, that just - *is* ... That comes through, as I say, in a number of different ways.
So I wrote to Lulu, as if I was somehow speaking for God.
"They discovered me when they looked around at the world and thought it was really beautiful or really mysterious and wondered where it came from".
That's not to say that there might not be arguments for the existence of God from the way the world is, but more that people, in encountering the abundance of the world, just somehow feel the interlocking beautiful patterns of the world.

I feel that with this kind of thing - well, I feel it in another human presence, I feel love and Intelligence.
And I run my hand on the fabric and what I sense is something like love or intelligence.

And then, wondering where that comes from is again not a matter of simple cause and effect. I think a lot of damage has in a way been done over the years by people using the old analogy of the *Watch – Man*. You find a very sophisticated machine and you think all that had to be *made* by somebody.
That only gets it so far, only up to a point, because the really extraordinary thing is not finding a *machine* but being confronted with this abundance of interwoven life and wondering how does it all hang together, how could someone make a fabric I like that.

So that was the starting point.
And then I went on to say, again trying to speak for God
"They discovered me when they were very very quiet on their own and felt a sort of peace and love they haven't expected".
I put that in because it's not only as we react to the world around us but also as we learn to be alone with ourselves that we discover...

I think it was the philosopher Descartes who said.

'All the problems of the world come from our inability to sit quietly with ourselves for fifteen minutes'.

And looking around at some of the extraordinary figures in global politics at the moment most of the problems come from the fact that they can't subscribe to quietness.

And when you're quiet and you accept the quiet person that is there... then I don't have to impress anybody, I don't have to talk so as to get on top of the situation, I don't have to silence anybody else. I have the right to be there, to be silent just to be (you remember the saying 'Don't *do* things, just - stand'?). Crucial.

And I think for all sorts of people, not least for young people, it is a really life-giving thing to be told

'You don't have to impress anyone!'

Because at the present the two things that really pressure us, especially the younger generation, is trying to succeed in the world's terms - career and assets like that

- and maintaining your profile in the social media. So you, wonder what's left if you take those two things away.
With a lot of people, that's a panicky idea. But I think that when they stop at that and sit with it for a moment it's going to actually feel like a liberated state.
Because you exist, because you just *are*. This is well said in the Jewish and Christian traditions and Muslim traditions too - that you exist because God wants you to.
You exist because God wants your company and wants you to discover that, in the silence of not having anything to do or anyone to impress.
It's an aspect of what some Christians mean by 'justification by faith'. You just - trust.
So the quiet is crucial.
And I think the deepest and most lasting elements, in any religious tradition, are those that help you into that place where you can simply stand and absorb, and not feel that you have to 'succeed', feel the peace and the peace of when you're on

your own and you've got over the pain barrier of not being able to impress people.

You can't actually love yourself into life, you have to be loved. And love yourself too.

Yes, that is the hardest. And as I say I don't think we can just do it in the abstract, we need others, especially we need to know that it's love that is the rationale for being here at all. That unless God's act of creation is an act of love nothing at all makes sense.

2

Beginning and continuing

That letter to Lulu had a lot of background, a lot of things lurking beneath each sentence. So let me use the rest of this bit of writing now in front of you to try to uncover some of them, leaving the rest for you to unscramble and discover, maybe in a better way than here, for yourself.

To start at the beginning (the beginning for me that is): how did I come into my - I won't call my 'profession' - my calling? Where did that come from?

I'm not surprised you're wondering, many people do.

I don't think it had much to do with my parents. It was a lot to do with belonging to a very active and welcoming church that was *there*. That was important to me.

Not initially the Church of England. We went to the local Presbyterian Church. It had a really gifted, very intellectually alert, minister with creative excellent services.

Even as a little boy I could tell that. And there was a strong feeling that churches were a place where you could, as it were, spread your wings.

Then when we moved to another town we started going to the Anglican Church (that is, the church in Wales), because there wasn't a Presbyterian church nearby.

And blessedly I found exactly the same atmosphere there, with another brilliant minister, a priest who really was somebody, deeply loved and admired, and he left that imprint on me. He was someone who also gave you the impression that Christianity was something that could expand your mind and your heart.

He loved poetry and drama too. It all came back to the moments when you saw him early in the morning kneeling in front of the altar and you knew where the centre was. A wonderful man.

I began to think seriously that I would really like to be like him - not really able to do *that* perhaps, but that there might be a role for a teacher and a pastor that I could step into.

It took me a long time to sort it all out but that's where it started I think, with a couple of brilliantly good examples.

And with it, the sense that the Christian faith was, in the words of the Psalms, 'you have not given me into the hands of the enemy but have set my feet in a large room'.

And as part of it, it should be a good room for females too.

And there is so much just from things you might think are merely 'ordinary'. Yes, all around us, including in songs you maybe hear every day, the singer Justin Bieber for instance, in the same way. Then again, a friend showed me this poem about - of all things – a drainpipe.

On a freezing February morning
With my window grudgingly open
I woke and saw through the crack
an unmistakable star.
I try various salutations
Such as Bright Star would I were

Steadfast as thou art etcetera
But gradually becoming more conscious
of the brute facts of matter
I remember that from my pillow
there is no view of the sky
I rise to inspect this wonder
only to find that my star
is a gleam on a black shiny drainpipe.
Sadly I turn back to bed
murmuring 'So you've caught me again
Plato you old magician
you think you've got me this time'.
Eppur
it was a star, a special kind
of star, an envoy from the depths
of space sent to me personally,
Its splendour reduced by reflection
to teach my awakening eyes
not the inferiority of Doxa
But the glorious ends to be served
by even a black drainpipe.

(Robert Murray SJ)

That and many everyday things remind us of the inscrutable ways in which a great problem can be presented. And when you think of stars themselves, what are they? Lumps of debris and rock waste. And yet and yet...

In Dante's *il paradiso* there's 'the love that moves the sun and other stars'. Love.

When you're called to be a priest you never know where you'll end up. Just as well! I think I'd assumed that I'd spend my ministry in teaching as well as pastoral work. Anyway, I have had a succession of jobs which allowed me to combine those two very happily, and then, to do it here and there.

After a time I was sent, to my surprise, to be Bishop in Wales - and the rest, well, the rest is history.

Photo of inauguration as archbishop??

Do I have any regrets?

Yes lots!

Of course. All kinds of regrets... I look back on decisions I've made and things that I've done. And also to some of my writing that could have been better, should be better.

But in terms of the course of my vocation as a pastor I have to say I don't regret that, or my being Archbishop. It was a very hard position to be in, certainly - but it had to be done and there was a lot of support. The strength of both human and divine resources have been a great grace.

But *now*, I've retired from that - to be in a completely different environment, and to be able to teach again, also just to concentrate on ministry in the church which doesn't have to be about administration or negotiation... I can... just *be*.

Just at 8 this morning, for example, I was in one of the local parish churches doing regular service for the parish. And the Sundays when I am not doing a service anywhere, that's fine too. I don't feel any homesickness at all for the grand years of the archbishopric.

And unlike Catholic priests, I didn't have to give up the idea of family and marriage. My wife is also a theologian and she helps to train clergy so she has a deep understanding of what it's all about. Her father also was a priest and a bishop.

When I was archbishop the greatest challenge was simply this - to keep people at the table together despite the deep divisions and the very heavy pressures from both sides of the controversy over sexuality - over gays. People were wanting a quick final solution and I didn't believe that there was going to be a quick solution because of the deep divisions.

But I really didn't want to lose anybody from the firm. That was a bit of a tightrope, to put it mildly. It was a way of guaranteeing that *nobody* would be really very pleased with what you were doing!

I think it was a matter of, as I say, just trying to keep people meeting and coming together. When we had the Lambeth Conference ten years ago I made the decision that we should begin with two days of retreat where we were to keep silence in the cathedral together with just a series of short addresses. The idea was that we wouldn't do any business during that time. We just prayed together and got to know each other in that quiet place. I think it helped to set the tone for the week that followed.

I am grateful for that.

The other thing I look back on is how in my last few years in office we did manage to put together a sort of coordinated plan for the entrance of the world. That was in terms of an engagement with relief and development issues so that lots of grassroots organisations and local organisations could be doing important relief work.

We created this thing called the Anglican Alliance, an umbrella organisation for development, engagement and advocacy. It brings together those in the Anglican family of churches and agencies to work for a world free of poverty, inequality and injustice, to raise the voices of the vulnerable, to reconcile those in conflict, and to safeguard the earth.

I was very pleased that we were able to set that up and see it start functioning. Something in the world.

3

Thinking, thoughts and things

I think the biggest challenge now is not about Christianity, religion or spirituality. It is in the deeply individualist approach which assumes that I am responsible for creating my being moment by moment. The whole cultural climate is so feverish and anxious about all that, I think that's where our biggest challenge lies. It's really *not* so much in the realm of religion and science, as some people think. I think *that* is a phoney war that can be dealt with.

The *real* thing is how we imagine ourselves as human, isn't it! That's what the thing is and that's why my last little book was called *Being Human.*

We need to get back to a *deeper* and *fuller* imagining of human beings' need to be individual. So the distinction I touched on in one chapter in that book was the difference between an individual and a person. An 'individual' is just a sort of lump, but an individual who is in a relationship is a *person*, connected.

The *word* 'consciousness' itself leads us to the same thing: it is *'con-sci-ousness'*: 'knowing together', connectedness. And the same in the Russian word сознание*(soznanue)* and in a number of other languages too. It's*community, communion*. And it's maybe not all centred just in the cognitive, in our conscious thinking.

There's an elderly nun that I've known for many years and that I see sometimes. I don't quite know whether she recognises me or not but I feel like she knows the sound of my voice somehow and its rhythms.

That reminds me that most religious traditions imagine creation as the first *sound*, the sound of words spoken. In Hinduism, the sacred syllable 'ohm' is pronounced at the beginning of all things. It is intriguing too that the names of God and so many God's have that primal quality, a breathed *sound* - Yahweh, Allah, Jehovah, Elohim... It is as if every time we

breathe we breathe the very name of God.
I think there's a real connection actually between the notion of the origins of language, speech, and the understanding of God.
Music too.

I think of the extraordinary insights and playing of Evelyn Glennie the percussionist. She came to speak here about 18 months ago with a series of talks on language and communication. She communicated the idea that we are *resonant*, so to speak, that we are vibrating in sympathy.
I think that that was something human being discovered right at the start. I picked up a book recently with the wonderful title of *The Singing Neanderthals*. Apparently the archaeological evidence we have of the cranial formation of Neanderthals suggests they had the capacity to make music, they had vocal cords in the space where music comes, before speech even,

so it came from how people literally resonated with one another.

4

Poems, poetry and how they happen

“They discovered me when they were very very quiet on their own and felt a sort of peace and love they hadn’t expected”
Yes, dear Lulu - that leads into poetry, another reverberating, sounding thing, very close to my heart.
Here are some of my own in which I try to capture some of the resonances of the created world, and its stillness (for how these poems happen for me, you will have to read on).
Since as I write this it is coming up to Christmas, that great moment, celebrated throughout the world, of the birth of a miraculous child, let me begin with this, arising from a particular time.

AdventCalendar
He will come like last leaf's fall.

One night when the November wind
has flayed the trees to the bone, and
earth
wakes choking on the mould,
the soft shroud's folding.

He will come like frost.
One morning when the shrinking earth
opens on mist, to find itself
arrested in the net
of alien, sword-set beauty.

He will come like dark.
One evening when the bursting red
December sun draws up the sheet
and penny-masks its eye to yield
the star-snowed fields of sky.

He will come, will come,
will come like crying in the night,
like blood, like breaking,
as the earth writhes to toss him free.
He will come like child.

Other poems too come from the experience and feel of a particular time (one that surely you too know).

Six o'clock

As the bird
rise of the sky, the last sun
looking up gilds on the hollows
of the wings and afterthought of gift to
guests ignored and hurt but no
the bird rides up the sky eyes on the light.

When the sun
levels its sights across the grass
it packs the blades of little animals
so tight so heavy that you wonder
why they don't tumble over
Into the new uncompromising shadow,
into their inner dark.

Or a particular place

Third station

Fall. And between the grey air
and your stone back will run the stream

quick cold of weeping breath
the mind's sour spit of overnight
coating the broken skin against its load.

Lift. And between the stine's spine
and the sun's weight are caught
The leavings if the mind, the groundsthat
cloud the bottom of the heart, and shake
and bitter it, press to the sun your skin.

Turn. And between the weight of heaven
and self
rub small the crying grain and burst
the puckered gelid streams, windpipe the
press,
and mill our parching salt, our black and
needful flour.
Bread. Tears.

How do I write these poems, how do they happen? Well, usually it is in one of two ways. Sometimes almost the whole poem arrives at once, and all I have to do is listen, to take it back. It just flows. I know this happens with some other poets too, but not everyone or not all the time.

More often I find it's a couple of images connecting some perceptions, and thinking that 'That belongs with that'. Or maybe a little phrase and I think 'Now where does it take us?'
Then I leave it for a bit. And then, later, I go back and, as you do, I kind of take the lid off and see if it's cooked and beautiful. That's often what it feels like.
Sometimes it can be months before it really comes together and I have to find the right moment when, as I said just now, it's time to take that lid off the hob and have a proper look and see if it's come yet.
But finding that right moment is very elusive.
Poems need to be *sounded*. For me, this reading aloud is the task of the poet.
Speaking of poetry, I must add that I dislike the idea of being 'a religious poet' as I am sometimes called. I would prefer to be called a poet for whom religious

things matter intensely. I like it that my poetry has been described as 'visionary yet earth-rooted' with ‘a genius for embodying abstract ideas’.

In fact, my poems are about many different things. They visit the Holy Land, commemorate the deaths of parents and close friends, explore elements of ancient Celtic culture... They’re inspired by works of art, landscapes rural and urban, and historical figures from Tolstoy to Simone Weil. What connects poem to poem is what has been called my ‘poetic and vividly sensual language’, trying to address, specifically and particularly, what matters most intensely.

I have to say - remember my upbringing - that my poems are deeply shaped by a sensibility shaped by Wales and by the Welsh language. They show the reality of the ‘bright, inner freedom' we can exercise through grace, even in a world whose gravity is all about us. I try to avoid the merely personal: the world exists and imagination and faith work together to explore and celebrate what is and what might be.

Headwaters is my third collection of poems, shot through, as they say, with complexity and passion. The poems range widely in subject, place and mood. I visit a martyrs' memorial and a prison in Uganda, meditate on the story of St Serafim of Sarov at the rock where 'at night Serafim knelt on the same rock, three long years', hear Bach's miraculous *St Matthew Passion*, to be 'exhausted with new grief, old treacheries, the view without prospect'. I reflect on the rivers of life, from their headwaters to the sea, and on landscapes and townscapes.

Poetry happens at a sort of junction in the mind when new combinations start-up, words and pictures start connecting in unexpected ways.

It takes you into what can feel like anarchic territory, and that's one reason for trying to give it some ballast by forms and structures.

Several of the poems I've chosen are about birth, one way or another - about the start of new life with all its dangers. But I've also chosen a couple that are a bit like incantations, reminding us of that aspect of poetry that is a bit like magic spells. And, to stop us being too solemn about it, a little light relief too.

Poetry is about discovery. Not with making it up but with listening, understanding my mind.

The same might be said by many people who write poetry. You don't just sit down and make it up you listen and listen, very very hard. And you wait for words.

There are a lot of folktales in Wales about how poetry comes, like the need to spend the night on a mountaintop. And in Ireland there are stories of how you had to compose poetry when in a coffin or submerged in water with one nostril exposed. A disorienting experience - when you somehow pick up the frequency you're otherwise not attached to.

I think that that's a key thing really. Our normal consciousness tunes into only a limited bandwidth and when we're disoriented in some way we simply pick up more, yes that's very important.

And my own favourites?

Well, we all have our own favourites, born out of, well, out of somewhere. Here are some of them. And a bit about why I like them and what I learn from them (as possibly you do too but maybe not for the same reasons).

I'll focus on the ones connected to the river that for some years I lived by and love.

Earth has not anything to show more fair:
Dull would he be of soul who could pass by
A sight so touching in its majesty:
This City now doth like a garment wear
The beauty of the morning: silent, bare,
Ships, towers, domes, theatres, and temples lie
Open unto the fields, and to the sky,
All bright and glittering in the smokeless air.
Never did sun more beautifully steep
In his first splendour valley, rock, or hill;
Ne'er saw I, never felt, a calm so deep!

The river glideth at his own sweet will:
Dear God! the very houses seem asleep;
And all that mighty heart is lying still!

As you see, I can't resist beginning with the great scene setter, Wordsworth, writing from Westminster Bridge near where I used to live.

It's a poem about stillness.

All poetry begins from that moment of stillness. Something in your environment, something in your language, something in your own experience brings you up short, and you don't quite know what to say but you have to work very hard to say it, all the same.

That moment of stillness, that moment of what I might call a "rest", is where the energy of poetry comes from. It's a paradox but a real one. Poetry comes from the experience of being shut up, being silenced. For Wordsworth it was looking out over a still morning scene. Nothing happening and yet that very nothing, demanding that we find a response to it.

But of course, poetry is generated by other kinds of borderland experience, other kinds of frontier experience. It's generated by facing love at a certain depth; by facing death and suffering at a certain depth. And in the poems I love I hear those different moments of being stilled or caught up suddenly, not knowing what to say, those are the moments at the heart of the imaginative experience.

Let me recall, predictably, a man by the name of William Shakespeare, whose work may be known to some of you. In the Sonnets, he explores a whole variety of ways in which love and death alike bring us up short and squeeze out of us things to say we didn't know we had to say.

Shakespeare, they say, knew quite a bit about the theatre and the Sonnet I want to start with begins with a very poignant and immediate theatrical image by which Shakespeare begins to find his way into speaking out of the silence and the stammering that generates poetry.

Sonnet 23 by William Shakespeare

As an unperfect actor on the stage,
Who with his fear is put beside his part,
Or some fierce thing replete with too much rage,
Whose strength's abundance weakens his own heart;
So I, for fear of trust, forget to say
The perfect ceremony of love's rite,
And in mine own love's strength seem to decay,
O'ercharg'd with burthen of mine own love's might.
O! let my looks be then the eloquence
And dumb presagers of my speaking breast,
Who plead for love, and look for recompense,
More than that tongue that more hath more express'd.
O! learn to read what silent love hath writ:
To hear with eyes belongs to love's fine wit.

"To hear with eyes" - Shakespeare is talking about one of those emotional frontier moments: stumbling, stammering in the context of human love that overwhelms, not knowing what to say. Love is one of those things which, if you find the words and imagination for it, somehow carries you round or through or over a fear of death. Poetry is one of those things that you invoke to silence some of the terrors that human experience gives you.

And so poetry is a kind of immortality, and odd sort of immortality and yet, because it's not confined, not penned in by the losses that time brings, surely it must have something to say that's relevant to a wider perspective where death doesn't just draw all mummeries.

Sonnet 60 by William Shakespeare

Like as the waves make towards the pebbled shore,
So do our minutes hasten to their end;
Each changing place with that which goes before,
In sequent toil all forwards do contend.
Nativity, once in the main of light,

Crawls to maturity, wherewith being crowned,
Crooked eclipses 'gainst his glory fight,
And Time that gave doth now his gift confound.
Time doth transfix the flourish set on youth
And delves the parallels in beauty's brow,
Feeds on the rarities of nature's truth,
And nothing stands but for his scythe to mow:
And yet to times in hope, my verse shall stand
Praising thy worth, despite his cruel hand.

One of the great things about the Sonnets is that Shakespeare has a thoroughly immodest view of what his poetry means and is about. It's an odd thing about poets that they are at one level deeply humbled by the patterns in what they say – they don't know quite where it comes from or where it's going to, and they don't quite know whether they can manage what's coming through.

At the same time, they have the confidence that they say what needs saying, and that's all you can say... That's the proper immodesty of poetry – this is how it is. "I don't know if this is poetry or not", said one substantial 20th Century poet, "but that's how it comes to me".

Shakespeare's immodesty in that sense is bearable I suppose, as we read the Sonnets, it doesn't sound like arrogance, simply because the poetry, again and again, would turn to the sense of brokenness that lies at the heart of it. The brokenness of feelings of betrayal which run right through the Sonnets as they run through so much of his greatest drama.

Borderland experiences, love and hate, passion and disgust mingling together interwoven so painfully in that Sonnet, as in many others.

It's not surprising that Shakespeare looking at himself wonders what it is that, in the human constitution, keeps life alive and trust alive, and something in that sense of self, something which, in Shakespeare's own case has a kind of religious aura around it and yet isn't conventionally a religious, that comes through.

Not only in the sense that what he said overcomes and goes beyond death: that there's something in humanity itself, in the human self, that is not wrapped up and stifled and tidied away even by death.

Somewhere in all of that lies the life of the soul; lies that which death doesn't stifle.

Moving along the riverbank a little way, we come across to one of the more celebrated medical students of the South Bank, a man named John Keats.

Keats was as preoccupied as Shakespeare with death but in a very different way. The death, the suffering he encountered in his medical studies but also the mortality which was vivid and physical for him, day after day, as someone who knew he was doomed to an early death.

In some of his poems, Keats directly addresses this question of mortality.

When I have Fears that I May Cease to Be by John Keats

When I have fears that I may cease to be,
Before my pen has gleaned my teeming brain,
Before my high-piled books, in charact'ry,
Hold like rich garners the full-ripened grain;
When I behold, upon the night's starred face,
Huge cloudy symbols of a high romance,
And think that I may never live to trace
Their shadows, with the magic hand of chance;
And when I feel, fair creature of an hour,
That I shall never look upon thee more,
Never have relish in the faery power
Of unreflecting love; -- then on the shore
Of the wide world I stand alone and think
Till love and fame to nothingness do sink.

You may already have noticed that the imagery of standing on the shore is around a good deal in some of these poems.

A riverbank isn't, necessarily, a safe or cosy place to be. And, of course, in much literature, crossing rivers is one of those central symbols for death. You stand on the shore, you look across and you're not quite sure what there is on the other side. Even if standing on the South Bank of the Thames, it all looks very, very solid on the other side there; some kind of political institution, I think, you may nonetheless feel that there are intimations of mortality around in all this.

So Keats standing on that shore, waiting for things to dissolve, is at one and the same time staking his position on the shore. It matters to be here and to say this. And yet knowing that on the far side of that very deep and dark water you don't know what lies there.

Again and again with Keats you have that interweaving of the rich, positive sense of the imagination and the inescapable echoes of loneliness and loss and death that come back. And the sense of celebrating what's strange, looking out in amazement at what is strange and unmanageable, is also a kind of death for the self, trying to imagine it. I don't know how to get on top of this experience of what I see.

And at one and the same moment, there's an overwhelming extravagance of expression and the inner sense of loss and disorientation.

And then the rich disorientation engendered by Chapman's translation of Homer's great ever-living epic:

On first looking into Chapman's Homer by John Keats

Much have I travelled in the realms of gold,
And many goodly states and kingdoms seen;
Round many western islands have I been
Which bards in fealty to Apollo hold.
Oft of one wide expanse had I been told
That deep-browed Homer ruled as his demesne,
Yet did I never breathe its pure serene
Till I heard Chapman speak out loud and bold.

Then felt I like some watcher of the skies
When a new planet swims into his ken;
Or like stout Cortez when with eagle eyes
He stared at the Pacific -- and all his men
Looked at each other with a wild surmise
–Silent, upon a peak in Darien.

Strange landscape, exhilarating, frightening, forlorn. All of those things and all of them bringing to silence, like stout Cortez's colleagues, all of them urging to the speech that comes on what one modern Polish poet called the "other side of silence".

But if these are exotic landscapes, it's important not to forget the way in which the familiar, the appallingly familiar landscapes, generate poetry and silence and passion; and the fear of engaging with death as well.

Coming to one of the most local poets of all, still further along the river, we start listening to William Blake.

Blake is, among many other things, the poet of the London back streets, the London gutters. Blake is the poet of the horrific, eviscerating experience of witnessing a poverty which in his own age is barely noticed.

Blake writes about London but he writes about that in the context of a much broader vision of what imagination is. He writes about the sufferings of children working in London; two poems about young chimney sweeps.

I can, for instance, the richly acoustic poem, *London* from *Songs of Experience*, followed by one of those much more ambitious and difficult bits from *The Four Zoas* about imagination and poverty and suffering.

London by William Blake

I wandered through each chartered street,
Near where the chartered Thames does flow,
A mark in every face I meet,
Marks of weakness, marks of woe.

In every cry of every man,
In every infant's cry of fear,
In every voice, in every ban,
The mind-forged manacles I hear:

How the chimney-sweeper's cry
Every blackening church appals,
And the hapless soldier's sigh
Runs in blood down palace-walls.

But most, through midnight streets I hear
How the youthful harlot's curse
Blasts the new-born infant's tear,
And blights with plagues the marriage-hearse.

The Four Zoas by William Blake
What is the price of Experience? Do men buy it for a song,
Or Wisdom for a dance in the street? No! it is bought with the price
Of all that a man hath -- his house, his wife, his children.
Wisdom is sold in the desolate market where none come to buy,
And in the wither'd field where the farmer ploughs for bread in vain.
It is an easy thing to triumph in the summer's sun,
And in the vintage, and to sing on the waggon loaded with corn:

It is an easy thing to talk of patience to the afflicted,
To speak the laws of prudence to the houseless wanderer,
To listen to the hungry raven's cry in wintry season,
When the red blood is fill'd with wine and with the marrow of lambs:
It is an easy thing to laugh at wrathful elements;
To hear the dog howl at the wintry door, the ox in the slaughter-house moan;
To see a God on every wind and a blessing on every blast;
To hear sounds of Love in the thunderstorm that destroys our enemy's house;
To rejoice in the blight that covers his field, and the sickness that cuts off his children,
While our olive and vine sing and laugh round our door, and our children bring fruits and flowers.
Then the groan and the dolour are quite forgotten, and the slave grinding at the mill,

And the captive in chains, and the poor in the prison, and the soldier in the field
When the shatter'd bone hath laid him groaning among the happier dead:
It is an easy thing to rejoice in the tents of prosperity --
Thus would I sing and thus rejoice; but it is not so with me.

Poetry is not simply celebration. Celebration alone, for Blake, belongs with those who have an easy place in which to live. And what comes from simply living in an easy place is not poetry as far as he is concerned.

Poetry emerges here from anger, from the awareness of hurt, from being diminished by the pain of someone else and finding in poetry words for your own diminution that will somehow serve to focus on the loss and the pain of another.

That means of course that the human heart itself is a very complicated thing. Out of it comes this impulse to poetry. A poetry of profound compassion. A poetry that looks towards transforming imagination.

But at the same time where else are the roots of evil except in the same human heart? And some of Blake's most powerful, epigrammatic poetry is about that dual character of the human heart, something which poetry alone can't resolve. He writes about the growth in the human heart of destructiveness and rivalry. Like some vast tree growing from the smallest seeds of resentment or rivalry.

Here are two of his most impassioned imaginings of that growth of evil in the heart.

Poison Tree by William Blake

I was angry with my friend:
I told my wrath, my wrath did end.
I was angry with my foe:
I told it not, my wrath did grow.

And I watered it in fears,
Night and morning with my tears;
And I sunned it with smiles,

And with soft deceitful wiles.

And it grew both day and night,
Till it bore an apple bright.
And my foe beheld it shine.
And he knew that it was mine,

And into my garden stole
When the night had veiled the pole;
In the morning glad I see
My foe outstretched beneath the tree.

And

The Human Abstract by William Blake
Pity would be no more
If we did not make somebody Poor;
And Mercy no more could be
If all were as happy as we.

And mutual fear brings peace,
Till the selfish loves increase:
Then Cruelty knits a snare,
And spreads his baits with care.

He sits down with holy fears,
And waters the grounds with tears;
Then Humility takes its root
Underneath his foot.

Soon spreads the dismal shade
Of Mystery over his head;
And the Caterpillar and Fly
Feed on the Mystery.

And it bears the fruit of Deceit,
Ruddy and sweet to eat;
And the Raven his nest has made
In its thickest shade.

The Gods of the earth and sea
Sought thro' Nature to find this Tree;
But their search was all in vain:
There grows one in the Human Brain.

If we want to understand the world we live in, I suspect that those two last poems of Blake tell us more than any number of political analyses.

What the tree is that grows in the human brain, that feeds on rivalry; that creates suffering so that it may have an opportunity for compassion; that secretes poison for the sake of revenge.

All of that seems to me a sadly accurate description of the world most of us have learned to inhabit. And listening to Blake is at least a reminder that that is not natural, however usual it may be, so long as the imagination continues to revolt against it.

And that, of course, is why Blake is a revolutionary. Not because he had a systematic, political program but because he believed, extraordinarily, that imagination changes things if you allowed it to work long enough.

And yet – it's a big "and yet" – the duality of the human heart remains.

Blake wrote two poems about the human heart and the divine image in the human heart and the negative image of the divine in the human heart. And we'll finish our sojourn with Blake by listening to those two poems.

The Divine Image (from Songs of Innocence) by William Blake

To Mercy, Pity, Peace, and Love
All pray in their distress;
And to these virtues of delight
Return their thankfulness.

For Mercy, Pity, Peace, and Love
Is God, our father dear,
And Mercy, Pity, Peace, and Love
Is Man, his child and care.

For Mercy has a human heart,
Pity a human face,
And Love, the human form divine,
And Peace, the human dress.

Then every man, of every clime,
That prays in his distress,
Prays to the human form divine,
Love, Mercy, Pity, Peace.

And all must love the human form,
In heathen, Turk, or Jew;
Where Mercy, Love, and Pity dwell

There God is dwelling too.

And

A Divine Image (from Songs of Experience) by William Blake

Cruelty has a human heart,
And Jealousy a human face;
Terror the human form divine,
And Secrecy the human dress.

The human dress is forged iron,
The human form a fiery forge,
The human face a furnace sealed,
The human heart its hungry gorge.

How is one to fathom the human heart? Imagination remains an act of faith. Imagination tells you not what is and not even what might be, but somehow what needs to be.

There's an element for every poet of necessity in what he or she says. As I said earlier, the poet doesn't simply say, "you might say it this way" or "here's a thought". The poet says,

"I can't *not* say this."

And that, "I can't not say this" is where the pressure, the integrity of poetry comes from. Poetry loses its integrity when it's either trying to be clever or trying to get a message across with a capital "m". '

That doesn't mean that poetry is uninterested in morality. You've just been listening to Blake and there's no more moral poet in the English language than William Blake. But as soon as poetry becomes a rhyming version of good advice it loses its energy. It loses its sense of necessity.

Blake as you will have seen, as you know, had a rather idiosyncratic approach to religion. And although he was for some of his life a neighbour to Lambeth Palace, I have a rather strong suspicion that he wasn't a very good neighbour to Lambeth Palace or rather that he thought, not without reason, that Lambeth Palace was not a very good neighbour to him! Or to any of those people about whom and for whom he most deeply wrote!

Having in the last years spoken about Blake on a couple of occasions, I have a very strong twinge of conscience as to what on earth Blake would have thought of an Archbishop of Canterbury talking about him. Neighbour or no neighbour in Lambeth, I think he would have been a little bit sceptical.

However, even Archbishops of Canterbury have an imagination somewhere and I want, in concluding this chapter, to pick up some of the themes I've been talking about and share with you two poems about borderlands.

A bit about death.

A bit about life.

A bit about standing on the shore, since that's one of those images that come back again and again.

I'll begin with a poem written in the middle '90's. It's a poem in memory of a friend of mine, Gillian Rose, a great philosopher who died on the ninth of December 1995.

I was travelling to visit her in hospital that day and arrived to find that she'd died just a little while earlier and that to the considerable surprise of myself and many of her friends, she'd been baptized on her deathbed. A very passionate and articulate Jew, she had finally made a journey that puzzled, bewildered, offended some, but found herself at last at home in a place she'd never expected to be.

The poem, *Winterreise...* [winter-journey] falls into three sections: morning, afternoon and night. Shaped by a train journey on a very foggy winter morning up through Gloucester in the Midlands towards Coventry, and an extremely disruptive journey back, sitting around in Swindon for what felt like an eternity because, thanks to the events of the day, I'd missed all the connections I'd planned.

Winterreise: for Gillian Rose, 9 December 1995

Morning

The flat fields tramp towards the Severn.

I know there is no cliff to drop from
their edge, only the sand and the wet still
sheets.
This morning, through, the thick and
chest-constricting
light, the level, rose-grey clouds and the
remains
of icy fog stand between fields and water.
And the horizon has to be a steep edge,
has to be
the cliff where Gloucester fell that never-
to-be measured
drop from his body to the ground.
And down, a long way down, below the
frost,
must be soft embers sending up the light
from fires the night-fog has muffled but
not killed.

Afternoon

Still, where you were concerned, we
always
arrived too late; too late, myopic, short of
sleep,
with fingers stumbling to decipher
messages

you left for us, engrave in a hard surface.
It was a distant relative of yours who
drove
his lawyer's reed into the black Sinai
basalt
till the calligraphy of little streams broke
out
to age the hopeless rock as if with history,
as if with words; another kinsman, distant
or not too distant,
writing in falling sweat on stone, body to
ground, something
his friends never quite managed to read.
Tracing, unthinkingly,
a pattern of spilled wine on the dayroom
table
never quite managing to meet each
other's eyes, or not for long,
we test the feel of an unyielding difficulty,
not yet sure
of handling this, of finding where the
streams combine,
reading what the wet fingertips decode.

Evening

Dying by degrees, perhaps is a winter
journey:
connections cancelled unexplained, the
staff,
their patience ebbing, closing amenities,
one by one, around you.
The temperature falls, and for an hour you
sit
on a plastic bench, aching for sleep,
under the surly light that strips you
For some always-delayed inspection; so
even,
so hard, that for so long you cannot see
the dark:
the homely dark, with its fierce small fires.

And a bit more recently, here is a poem not exactly based on, but certainly inspired by, an enormously long medieval Welsh poem on the great pilgrimage centre in Chester of the Middle Ages where a great wonder working crucifix was set up, the Rood of Chester.
The legend was that this huge crucifix had landed on the shore at Chester. It had been found one morning on the sand

outside of Chester. And the legend developed that it was actually made out of fragments of the true cross or embodied fragments of the true cross, that it had drifted all the way to Chester from Jerusalem, geography not being one of the strong points in the Middle Ages.

And this great wonder working crucifix, the centre of pilgrimage in North Wales and the northwest of England was, of course, cut down and destroyed in the Reformation, chopped up and for a while used in one of the local grammar schools as the whipping block.

Seashores evoke all kinds of things. They evoke the wooden horse of Troy on the shore outside the walls of the city. They evoke some of the legends about the true cross. The amazingly vivid imagery that this particular medieval poet uses about the gull's table, the sea as the gull's table, where the food is spread by God and an imagery drawn from Welsh mythology of the wounded eagle who figures in one of the great prose romances of the Middle Ages.

The Rood of Chester (after
GruffyddapMeredudd)
Cut from the flowering tree,
the body sails by night
over a scouring sea,
stained by red white.

Monday at dawn, between the walls and the sand,
they saw the carpenter's masterpiece, delivered
out of the winter country on crowned waves.
The clouds' siege lifted and the rain sailed home.
Polished as bone, the oak comes through the storm
alive, fingered and pressed by winter after winter,
rolled on the gulls' table till it swims clear
between the walls and the sand at dawn.
They climbed down from the walls to see
the winter's carpentry, the skills of a far-off land

where they speak only the gulls' tongue;
they walked
the noisy strand, one eye still on the white
waves.,
One eye on the wind's knives. What else
has winter
to deliver? The oak is spread like wings,
an eagle five times speared as it drops
out of winter between the walls and the
sand.

From Adam's sandy grave
blossoms the magic rod,
stacked in the Temple's nave
to wait for the nails of God.

There is no gift like this for a city,
no wood but this for the roof, the bloodied
wings,
the salted timber. They hauled it from the
sand
and wrapped and hung it in the dense
rafters, singing.
And like that other image from the shore,
at night its belly cracked and the men
began

to scramble out, the men folded
into the eagle's wing, the men and women
devoured.
By its five hungry wounds. It has gathered
all who have left their walls, who were lost
in winter,
on whom the towns have closed their
doors;
they will make the foursquare City of the
Legions
A camp of little fires for the homeless
where they sing unfamiliar songs in the
gulls' tongue -
until the legions douse the hearths and
take the ground again
and carve the oak into a whipping block
for bad boys.

When the children weep
at their corrected fault
the clipped bird stirs in sleep
tasting remembered salt.

Well, those are some of my favourites (you can see more if you wish at

http://aoc2013.brix.fatbeehive.com/articles.php/1752/rowan-williams-on-poetry/)
from poets from places clustered around the river - it's always good to be local - by which I for some time lived.

You surely have your own - different - favourite poems and lyrics too, worth thinking about.

5

Thinking and thoughts and Narnia

I don't know if you know the *Narnia* books? Maybe they're now out of fashion but I still read them. I was born the year the first one came out and like many other readers I have always found them a great resource for thinking and feeling.

Some people are quite surprised that I like C S Lewis, someone who perhaps looks like a cosy conservatist far removed from any kind of probing Christianity. But I was born in 1950, the same year as the first Narnia book was published and then at 14 or 15, as I was when I first read some of those books, and I felt 'Wow, we've got a clever man on our side! Isn't that good!'

Actually the theology grabbed me even before I'd got into the stories themselves, but when I properly read them as a student I found them astonishingly good – both as exciting adventures and religious writing.

As a child, I must have read the whole series through half-a-dozen times. But when a schoolmate pointed out to me the parallels between Aslan and Jesus, I felt cheated; it was as though Lewis was smuggling in propaganda.
By now I see *The Lion, the Witch and the Wardrobe* as very clearly a book about the life of Christ, in a way that isn't true of the others. It's such an obvious parallel. The more interesting thing, however, is how Lewis manages to convey a sense of what the religious climate, the religious sensibility might be in another world. That is the teasing thing.

Why turn Christ the lamb into Christ the lion? It's as if there's a feeling that something really quite fierce has taken hold of people when they turn to God. Myself, I've always connected this in my mind with T S Eliot's image of Christ the tiger in his poem *'Gerontion'* – something springs on you, even though fearsomeness is not a quality many people associate with the Church of England!

Not that my evangelical enemies ever see *me* as fierce! More likely as being too wishy-washy and open-minded – the same qualities that have led some secular intellectuals to claim me. And as one atheist put it: 'We know he secretly doesn't really believe in all that Jesus and God stuff. He just thinks they're excellent metaphors.

In my view both sides are fundamental misreadings. I am firmly convinced that Jesus's followers regarded him as divine long before the Council of Nicaea decreed it in 325. I think with awe of the divine life being clothed in human flesh and blood and am certain the tomb was empty.

Of all his works, I most admire the short book Lewis wrote after the death of his beloved wife Joy, *A Grief Observed* - a staggering book, far angrier than his other Christian writings.

When you are happy, Lewis writes, God welcomes you. 'But go to Him when your need is desperate, when all other help is vain, and what do you find? A door slammed in your face, and a sound of bolting and double bolting on the inside. After that, silence'.

Remarkably, similar struggles are present in Narnia. In *The Silver Chair*, a witch has imprisoned the marsh-wiggle Puddleglum with Eustace and Jill. She tries to persuade them the world above ground is only a fantasy. The children are ready to give in but Puddleglum resists: 'I'm on Aslan's side even if there isn't any Aslan to lead it'. These lines seem remarkably close to the theories of some modern theologians who hold that the truth of religious language is not as important as how useful it is in everyday life.

Are we back to the idea of God being a metaphor?

No! Puddleglum's statement of faith isn't saying it doesn't matter whether it's true or not. He's saying I have no means of knowing whether this is or isn't true… But I know there's something here that I can't let go of without letting go of myself.

I see Lewis as like St John of the Cross, the Spanish mystic who went through a dark night of the soul but came through to see the light of truth. Lewis thought most theologians were gutless liberals who didn't care about the truth enough.

("Gutless liberals"? Maybe you know some, yes? Maybe even you? So *are* they necessarily gutless?)

One of the most vivid scenes comes in *The Voyage of the Dawn Treader* when Eustace – the spoiled child of non-smoking teetotal vegetarians: never a good sign in Lewis – is turned into a dragon. He tries to peel off his skin but finds only another set of scales. It takes Aslan to cut his claws in deep and rip it off – a "feeling worse than anything I've ever felt", as Eustace says – for him to be reborn.

Isn't this astonishing. We are all of us human beings in love with fictions about ourselves – dramas in which we star. And because Lewis was a big dramatic character himself, I think he knew it as well as anyone. But self-examination only takes you so far. Eventually Eustace has to turn to Aslan and say – go on, you do the job. He finds layers he never knew he had being stripped away.

Most children, I imagine, miss the allegory; but most respond to story and to Aslan's vital sensuousness, which you can almost see as being on the knife-edge of the erotic.

The same in *The Lion* when Lucy and Susan roll around in the grass with the big cat. You can see from his writing that Lewis has a very strong sense of physical pleasures - including the pleasure of a pint in the pub, which he notoriously celebrates on many occasions.

The Narnia books were written in a very different era from our own and are now attacked for being misogynist – remember that notorious moment when Susan is excluded from Narnia because of loving "nylons and lipsticks and invitations"! – and even racist. Aslan's swarthy enemies the Calormens speak like parodies of *Arabian Night's characters* and worship Tash – a bizarre concoction of Babylonian devil and Hindu god. Lewis wrote in his letters that *The Horse and His Boy* showed "the calling and conversion of the heathen". Some have even pointed out that the White Witch tempts Edmund with *Turkish* Delight!

I wouldn't deny any of this. They are of their era. I remember, though, that in *The Last Battle* we meet a Calormene soldier called Emeth. All his life he has served the diabolical Tash and when he confronts Aslan you might expect him to be cast into hell. Instead Aslan says "unless thy desire had been for me, thou wouldst not have sought so long and so truly" (that's a near direct quotation from St Augustine), and brings him into heaven.

Here is someone with total courage, passion and generosity who's giving all that to a mistaken target. But the heavenly postman knows better and delivers it to the right address.

Isn't that nice?

I should add that for me Christianity is paramount, for me no other religions are equivalent to Christianity. All the same grace is everywhere, it turns up in unexpected places. What about people who serve oppressive governments or work in morally compromised professions? Can you occupy any position of authority and remain untainted?

Right, there are controversies here. But these are ones on which the church has to be attentive and to speak out, even if it is deeply unpopular – like saying that aspects of Islamic *sharia* will inevitably become part of British law, or describing the Big Society as "aspirational waffle".

But important as that might be, in the end it is the spiritual message, the deeper questions, that matter.

Great writers like Lewis provoke you into looking beyond yourself. They seem to say: "Do you recognise that? Does that ring a bell? Something is moving in on you – well, getting its claws into you". Listen World!

And there are so many things in the world to inspire us - for us, as the great percussionist Evelyn Glennie tells us, to 'reverberate to'.

6

A Prison Visit

I recall a visit to Grendon prison. Coming through the bars and bolts
The window inside was thick and whorled, impossible to see through; the panes were separated not by lead but thick concrete, in circles rather smaller than a man could squeeze through.

[INSERT PRISON FENCE PICTURE]

The ushers were broad-shouldered men in pressed shirts standing quietly against the walls.
The men who entered were silent and seemed tired as if they had walked a long way from someplace fashion had never reached. A couple wore rosaries or crosses. Two or three looked hard, with tattoos and sharp muscles.
The only way to get a feeling for what goes on is to be exposed to it, so what they did was to sit me down, as they do to

most visitors, as if I was a part of a therapy group. They sat round in a loose circle on plain chairs just like mine.

It didn't seem right to pray, rather I just listened. They began to introduce themselves, exactly as they would if I was a new inmate.

"I'm doing life for murder, coming off a drug episode. Welcome to Grendon."

"I've been 34 years, inside. Doing life for murder, been here before. I have difficulties dealing with people in authority. Welcome to Grendon."

"I'm doing life for killing my girlfriend. I come here to understand myself and why I chose certain routes to get here. Welcome to Grendon."

"I'm doing two life sentences. This really is hard. Welcome to Grendon" - this was from a young man with arched eyebrows, large, deep-set eyes and a look of sincerity and pain.

"Indecent assault. ..."

“Attempted murder”

“Been here three years. Second time”...

When they had introduced themselves they asked me questions.
“How do you get to be Archbishop of Canterbury?”
"By being very wicked in a previous life”.

When the laughter had died down I gave a careful explanation of the process, which managed to be thoroughly confusing until a Catholic prisoner said: "So you're elected, like the pope?"
“Yes - though the pope doesn't have a prime minister to worry about."
I went on to enumerate the five levels that I thought composed the job, from being the bishop for east Kent to being a kind of president of the worldwide family of Anglican churches, so that I tried to visit where churches were in trouble. To me the most important and worthwhile of these jobs was the least in the eyes of the world: being a diocesan bishop in east Kent (the other half of Kent was looked after by the Bishop of Rochester). As for the bit that was supposedly running the Church of England, that, I explained, was

basically meetings, paperwork, and decisions about money.

Then someone raised the royal wedding, wanting to know how I coped with all the attention.

I explained that It's essentially about the habits you try to form: making time every day to be quiet with God. That's what I am answerable to. It's very important to settle yourself and to remind myself that this is a time that God gives me, not just a time I give to God.

For me prayer is a matter of trying to clear a space in my head so that

I engage in this daily prayer in a very careful, practical way, almost as if it was therapy: I try to breathe regularly, sit upright, breathe, and say some simple words. I will often say 'Lord have mercy' slowly, at intervals, and just let it settle into my stomach.

It doesn't always seem to work. Sometimes I can be there for half an hour and the thoughts just go galloping round like horses in the Grand National. Then I have to remind myself again that this is time God gives to me, and not just time I give to God. It's as if you're trying to open the cellar door and be aware of the darkness underneath the water.

Another prisoner asked about "the whatever it is upstairs, where you've got quite a pull" (I supposed he meant the House of Lords or the government, not heaven): "Do you believe that the MPs and so on who talk about social exclusion know anything about it at all?"

"Good question", I had to reply. "I'm a bit sceptical that they do... I think that prison ought to be about equipping people to be what they have got it in them to be. What if prisons were really like that?"

Grendon, so far as possible, actually is like that, not an ordinary prison. It is a unique experiment within the prison system, which has been going for 50 years. In Grendon, prisoners are all members of a therapeutic community as well. The prisoners must work with themselves, with each other, and with the staff to address the causes of their wrongdoing. They have to talk about who they are, and why they came there, in the hope that they can change and in future keep out.

Talking about such things is a sign of dangerous “weakness” in most of the rest of the prison system. But "this place runs on honesty and truth", said one prisoner. "If something ever happened to you then it has happened to other group members."

One of the prisoners said in the introduction session that the biggest surprise of the prison had been what had happened to him:

"From the age of 10 I had just stuck two fingers up at society. I hated the world. But if you are honest with yourself and make yourself vulnerable you will change."

It doesn't work for everybody. Peter Bennett, the governor, a stocky forceful man with an air of melancholy, describes his success in terms that sound self-deprecating until you realise what they imply about some other prisoners. "We have very little self-harm. Very little bullying; a very low incidence of drugs – sometimes none. Grendon does make a difference."

He doesn't claim anything like complete success. "We see – not stunning, not incredible – but meaningful improvements. Grendon is essentially and profoundly a humane prison: the underlying humanity is embedded in bricks and mortar. It is a place where people behave with great respect to one another."

There were prisoners even in the group I saw who were back inside for the second time. But there is something remarkable going on there. The great trick is to run a democratic therapeutic committee inside a hierarchical prison. We have to allow a space for therapy and balance that with security.

True, the high fences around the prison are topped with barbed wire. Face it. And all visitors pass through a kind of security airlock.

This is a jail all right. The men are locked up all night and at lunchtime too. But they are treated as human beings, and encouraged to treat each other that way, too. They seem to respond.

"In other jails, staff didn't seem to have that much pride in their job," said one prisoner, "but they're not here just because they want the money".

"In the first carol service here I met the number one governor, Peter Bennett, and – he's all nice. [Laughter]. I was wondering what's that about. He sees you as a human being. It softens your heart."

It is exactly the kind of transformation that I most believe in. So when I prayed at the end of the meeting, I didn't mention sin or forgiveness but spoke of healing and honesty as things that all of us needed, without affectation.

Inth night f thus prayer

"O God, you know the difficulties we each face; you know when we feel trapped and alone.

Help us to remember that you love us and will never abandon us.

May we work with you to bind up the broken-hearted, and set the captives free, and proclaim freedom to the prisoner.
That all may know that they are loved and they are not alone".
It was only a visit, just trying to do what I could in a small way. Like you do, I believe in the power of localism, the small local things we can try to do.

7

Facing reality...

Obviously one has to recognise that religion is not always good for people. In fact some of the images and metaphors we use when talking about God are simply exaggerated versions of human-powered human control.

Also we project threatening emotions and thoughts onto God. Yes in that sense we *do* make God in our own image. And sometimes we make it in the image of our worst selves, not our best.

When I was working in a parish years ago one of the things which most came home to me was that it wasn't so much that I had to help people believe in God but quite often had to *stop* people believing in the God they thought they believed in, because it was such a bizarre and vindictive God.

I think it's important that religious people are honest about the ways in which it can go so badly wrong. So that's why in that letter to Lulu I went on to say that

"From time to time I sent them some hints especially in the life of Jesus to help them get closer to what I'm really like."

I'm speaking of course as a Christian who believes that the life and death and resurrection of Jesus is the place where we get the fullest insight, where we see *precisely* the God who as Jesus says does not come to be served but to serve, who does not impose power from outside but changes by speaking to the heart, going to the deepest most vulnerable places and starting from there.

Jesus doesn't come with an array of what you might call technological resource to get his way - the temptation: yes that's exactly what I'm meaning, because of course we all want quick solutions.

Jesus lives, it seems, and dies on the basis that the one thing that *can't* be forced is love or trust.

The great Russian theologian on whom I did research years ago, Vladimir Losski, apparently talked to one of his friends once about the old mediaeval riddle 'Can God make a stone too heavy for him to lift?' And what he said was 'Yes. The human heart'.

I know that some people, religious people, struggle to get their minds round the death of Christ, the suffering of the crucifixion, but are helped by a wonderful Shakespeare sonnet. It doesn't blink the searing, continuing, agony, that never goes away - as TS Eliot wrote 'People change and smile but the agony abides'. But the final couplet brings us, Shakespeare-wise, to the paradoxical resolution - the 'ransom' through love, tears.

It is not one of Shakespeare's better known sonnets but some think it one of his best.

Why didst thou promise such a beauteous day
And make me travel forth without my cloak,
To let base clouds o'ertake me in my way,
Hiding thy brav'ry in their rotten smoke?

'Tis not enough that through the cloud thou break,
To dry the rain on my storm-beaten face.
For no man well of such a salve can speak
That heals the wound and cures not the disgrace.
Nor can thy shame give physic to my grief;
Though thou repent, yet I have still the loss.
The offender's sorrow lends but weak relief
To him that bears the strong offense's cross.
Ah, but those tears are pearl which thy love sheds,
And they are rich, and ransom all ill deeds.

Shakespeare, Sonnet 34

(In Elizabethan pronunciation 'sheds' and 'deeds' rhyme)
Shakespeare has this extraordinary gift for summarising Christian doctrine. I've

been studying his *Measure for Measure* a bit, a wonderful play. That is such a serious summary of the doctrine of the Atonement. It is what Isabella says to Angelo

'Why all the souls that were, were forfeit once,
And he that best the vantage took
Found out the remedy'.

God has - so to speak - every advantage in terms of power, in terms of high ground. But he uses his freedom and power solely to bring healing.

It all comes back to this question of what models of God we have in our mind and allowing the reality of Christ to challenge the models we may have

So that's why I imagined God as saying.

"There was nothing and nobody around before me to invent me. It's like somebody who writes a story in a book I started making up the story of the world and eventually invented human beings like

you who could ask me awkward questions".
Like *you* do perhaps.
That idea that God creates and delights in the human mind is important. One of the worst things we can do when we speak of the mind is to let it be parked or silenced. The Episcopal Church in the United States used to have a poster advertising his existence which said

'He died to take away your sins not your mind'.

That's beautiful.
I guess it comes best into focus when I look at something like the Book of Job in the Bible because there you have one of the most brutal statements of the problem of suffering. In that book somebody is presented to you at the beginning who is completely innocent, and loses everything. But instead of just buckling down under it or looking for pious explanations he shakes his fist at God. Chapter after chapter after chapter, he just stands there and says to God "I need, I *need*, you to tell me what this is about!'.

And eventually God appears and says what he says at the end to the pious advisers, the killers

"You have not spoken well of me, as my servant Job has, as a human being exercising their mind fully and freely and not being afraid of God".

And God says "I *want* you to ask questions, I *want* you to have the courage to challenge me, I don't want a creation which is passive and compliant"

So it seems to me quite clear that the God we believe in is a god who encourages the questioner with courage as the challenger, who doesn't seem to be offended by us being a bit rude. It's a depressing picture of godliness, the idea that we have to see a God that is so delicate that he can't cope with challenge. We do no favours to God by imagining him as full of sensitivities.

And I think that's also why although blasphemy is offensive and unpleasant for Christians it's *our* problem not God's. The best that people can do is to make sure they're not just sitting passively. We should recall the great tradition of protest and probing in Christian and indeed in Jewish law, Luther too.

The truth is the writing about people who are in deep distress crying out 'Why is this happening and what do you think you're doing, *where the hell are you?*' - that writing has authenticity, reality.

Well that's something you're always discovering and rediscovering. I think that speaking about the centrality of love is not just sentimental or mollycoddling us. The thing about God's love is that it is absolutely creative in a reality that has its own integrity.

And of course my love of you or anyone else is going to be a pale shadow of that. But still you see it happening, the reality, when you love anyone.

In the churches we talk about 'sacraments', like for baptism or marriage or death. It's something that calls you back to the central reality by embodying it in some way. That's the sense in which *people* can be sacramental and if we have any blessings in our lives, in our

relationships, it's because other people have been sacramental, and those who have been blessed to have loving parents, that have living partnerships...
We know quite well that something of the selflessness that enriches you and makes your life is a shadow of that sharing endless love.
So - not a passive love, not unquestioned not accepting. You are *right*, Lulu to ask God 'awkward questions'.
And I think that *he* was right too, don't you, not to go all sensitive but to respond and challenge right back that
"Rather like somebody who writes a story in a book, I started making up the story of the world and eventually invented human beings like you who could ask me awkward questions!"
Too right!

8

Our precious world - thinking about environment and climate

Sometimes it's the young people who take a lead in reminding us of practical and moral issues. I think of the 'Long March of the Eco-Mad Youngsters' from Exeter Cathedral School, who completed a 90-mile pilgrimage to highlight their concerns about the environment.

Aged between 10 and 14, they were walking the ancient pilgrims' trail from Canterbury to London to highlight their petition for urgent government action to help prevent damaging climate change. I was glad to welcome them to Lambeth Palace and sign their petition which they then delivered to 10 Downing Street.

The children, who were accompanied on the walk by teachers and parents, had designed their own t-shirts to spell out their slogan 'ECO-MAD' ('Every Child's Opportunity to Make A Difference'). They had also created poems and artwork to convey their environmental themes.

The children can be rightly proud of what is a great achievement. They have taken on this huge task with immense determination, focus and spirit. We must act now, and act together, if we are to prevent permanent and irreversible damage being done to the planet.

The prayers and concerns for safe stewardship of God's Creation shown by these children sets a marvelous example for us all.

They are right, we have a responsibility for the earth, *our* earth, God will not step in to save us from our own folly, greed and neglect, we must act on our own.

Some modern philosophers have spoken about the human face as the most potent sign of what it is that we can't master or exhaust in the life of a human other – a sign of the claim upon us of the other, the depths we can't sound but must respect. And while it is of course so ancient a metaphor to talk about the "face" of the earth that we barely notice any longer that it is a metaphor, it does no harm to let some of these associations find their way into our thinking; because such associations resonate so strongly with a fundamental biblical insight into the nature of our relationship with the world we inhabit.

"The earth is the Lord's", says the 24th psalm. In its context, this is primarily an assertion of God's glory and overall sovereignty. And it affirms *a relation between God and the world* that is independent of what we as human beings think about the world or do to the world. The world is in the hands of another. The earth we inhabit is more than we can get hold of in any one moment or even in the sum total of all the moments we spend with it. Its destiny is not bound only to human destiny, its story is not exhausted by the history of our particular culture or technology, or even by the history of the entire human race.

We can't as humans *oblige* the environment to follow our agenda in all things, however much we can bend certain natural forces to our will; we can't control the weather system or the succession of the seasons. The world turns, and the tides move at the drawing of the moon. Human force is incapable of changing any of this.

What is before me is a network of relations and interconnections in which the relation to me, or even to us collectively as human beings, is very far from the whole story. I may ignore this, but only at the cost of disaster. And it would be dangerously illusory to imagine that this material environment will adjust itself at all costs so as to maintain our relationship to it. If it is more than us and our relation with it, it can survive us.

We are dispensable. But the earth remains the Lord's.

It’s a primary and defining relation: the core of a biblical ethic of responsibility for the environment. To understand that we and our environment are alike in the hands of God, so that neither can be possessed absolutely, is to see that the mysteriousness of the interior life of another person and the uncontrollable difference and resistance of the material world are connected. Both demand that we do not regard relationships centred upon us, upon our individual or group agendas, as the determining factor in how we approach persons or things. If, as this whole section of Leviticus assumes, God's people are called to reflect what God is like, to make God's holiness visible, then just or good action is action which reflects God's purpose of liberating persons and environment from possession and the exploitation that comes from it – liberating them in order that their "primary and defining relation" may be realised.

Just action, towards people and environment, is letting created reality, both human and non-human, stand before God unhindered by attempts to control and dominate.

It is a rather different reading of the biblical tradition to that often (lazily) assumed to be the orthodoxy of Judeo-Christian belief. We hear regularly that this tradition authorises the exploitation of the earth through the language in Genesis about "having dominion" over the non-human creation.

This is a very clumsy reading of what Genesis actually says. There humanity is given the task of "cultivating" the garden of Eden: we are not left simply to observe or stand back, but are endowed with the responsibility to preserve and direct the powers of nature. In this process, we become more fully and joyfully who and what we are – as St Augustine memorably says, commenting on this passage: there is a joy, he says, in the "experiencing of the powers of nature".

Our own fulfilment is bound up with the work of conserving and focusing those powers, and the exercise of this work is meant to be one of the things that holds us in Paradise and makes it possible to resist temptation.

The implication is that an attitude to work which regards the powers of nature as simply a threat to be overcome is best seen as an effect of the Fall, a sign of alienation. And, as the early scholar

Thomas Aquinas put, humanity takes part in the working of divine Providence because it has the task of using its reasoning powers to provide for self and others (both persons and things).

In other words, the human task is to draw out potential treasures in the powers of nature and so to realise the convergent process of humanity and nature discovering in collaboration what they can become. The "redemption" of people and material life in general is not a matter of resigning from the business labour and of transformation – as if we could – but the search for a form of action that will preserve and nourish an interconnected development of humanity and its environment.

In some contexts, this will be the deliberate protection of the environment from harm: in a world where exploitative and aggressive behaviour is commonplace, one of the "providential" tasks of human beings must be to limit damage and to secure space for the natural order to exist unharmed.

In others, the question is rather how to use the natural order for the sake of human nourishment and security without pillaging its resources and so damaging its inner mechanisms for self-healing or self-correction. In both, the fundamental requirement is to discern enough of what the processes of nature truly are to be able to engage intelligently with them.

All of this suggests some definitions of what unintelligent and ungodly relation with the environment looks like. It is *partial*: that is, it refuses to see or understand that what can be grasped about natural processes is likely to be only one dimension of interrelations far more complex than we can gauge. It focuses on aspects of the environment that can be comparatively easily manipulated for human advantage and ignores inconvenient questions about what less obvious connections are being violated.

It is indifferent, for example, to the way in which biodiversity is part of the self-balancing system of the world we inhabit.

It is impatient: it seeks returns on labour that are prompt and low-cost, without consideration of long-term effects. It avoids or denies the basic truth that the environment as a material system is finite and cannot indefinitely regenerate itself in ways that will simply fulfil human needs or wants.

And when such unintelligent and ungodly relation prevails, the risks should be obvious. We discover too late that we have turned a blind eye to the extinction of a species that is essential to the balance of life in a particular context. Or we discover too late that the importation of a foreign life-form, animal or vegetable, has upset local ecosystems, damaging soil or neighbouring life-forms. We discover that we have come near the end of supplies – of fossil-fuels for example – on which we have built immense structures of routine expectation. Increasingly, we have to face the possibility not only of the now familiar problems of climate change, bad enough as these are, but of a whole range of "doomsday" prospects.

Martin Rees's 2003 book, *Our Final Century,* outlined some of these, noting also that the technology which in the hands of benign agents is assumed to be working for the good of humanity is the same technology which, universally available on the internet, can enable "bio-terror", the threat to release pathogens against a population.

This feels like an ultimate reversal of the relation between humanity and environment envisaged in the religious vision – the material world's processes deliberately harnessed to bring about domination by violence; though, when you think about it, it is only a projection of the existing history of military technology.

AS Byatt's novel *The Biographer's Tale* tells the story – or rather a set of interconnected stories – of a writer engaging with the literary remains of a diverse collection of people, including Linnaeus, the great Swedish botanist. In the book Fulla, a Swedish entomologist

(expert on insects) holds forth to the narrator and his friends about the varieties of devastation the world faces because of our ignorance of insect life, specifically the life of bees. "She told fearful tales of possible lurches in the population of pollinators (including those of the crops we depend on for our own lives).
Tales of the destruction of the habitats by humans, and of benign and necessary insects, birds, bats and other creatures, by crop-spraying and road-building... Of the need to find other (often better) pollinators, in a world where they are being extinguished swiftly and silently. Of the fact that there are only thirty-nine qualified bee taxonomists in the world, whose average age is sixty... of population problems, and feeding the world, and sesbania, a leguminous crop which could both hold back desertification, because it binds soil, and feed the starving, but for the fact that no one has studied its pollinators or their abundance or deficiency, or their habits, in sufficient detail."

It is a potent catalogue of unintelligence. Earlier in the book Fulla has said that "We are an animal that needs to use its intelligence to mitigate the effects of its intelligence on the other creatures" – a notable definition in the contemporary context of what the Levitical call to redemption might mean. We cannot but use our intelligence in our world, and we are bound to use it, as Fulla's examples suggest, to supply need, to avoid famine and suffering. Intelligence is an aspect of sharing in God's Providence and so it is committed to providing for others.

But God's Providence does not promote the good only of *one* sector of creation; and so we have to use our intelligence to seek the good of the whole system of which we are a part. The limits of our creative manipulation of what is put before us in our environment are not instantly self-evident, of course; but what is coming into focus is the level of risk involved if we never ask such a question, if we collude with a social and economic order that apparently takes the possibility of unlimited advance in material prosperity for granted, and systematically ignores the big picture of global interconnectedness (in economics or in ecology)

Ecological questions are increasingly being defined as issues of *justice;* climate change has been characterised as a matter of justice both to those who now have no part in decision-making at the global level yet bear the heaviest burdens as a consequence of the irresponsibility of wealthier nations, and to those who will succeed us on this planet – justice to our children and grandchildren.

So the major issue we need to keep in view is how much injustice is let loose by any given set of economic or manufacturing practices. We can't easily set out a straightforward code that will tell us precisely when and where we step across the line into the unintelligence and ungodliness I have sketched. But we can at least see that the question is asked, and asked on the basis of a clear recognition that there is no way of manipulating our environment that is without cost or consequence – and thus also of a recognition that we are inextricably bound up with the destiny of our world.

There is no guarantee that the world we live in will "tolerate" us indefinitely if we prove ourselves unable to live within its constraints.

Is this – as some would claim – a failure to trust God, who has promised faithfulness to what he has made?

I think that to suggest that God might intervene to protect us from the corporate folly of our practices is as unchristian and unbiblical as to suggest that he protects us from the results of our individual folly or sin. This is not a creation in which there are no risks. The inexhaustible love of God cannot *compel* justice or virtue; we are capable of doing immeasurable damage to ourselves as individuals, and it seems clear that we have the same terrible freedom as a human race. God's faithfulness stands, assuring us that even in the most appalling disaster love will not let us go; but it will not be a safety net that guarantees a happy ending in this world... But to say this is also to be reminded of the fact that intelligence is given to us; we are capable of changing our situation – and, as ASByatt's character puts it, using our intelligence to limit the ruinous effect of our intelligence. If we can change things so appallingly for the worse, it is possible to change them for the better also. But, in Christian terms, this needs a radical change of heart, a conversion; it needs another kind of "redemption", which frees us from the trap of an egotism that obscures judgment. Intelligence in regard to the big picture of our world is no neutral thing, no simple natural capacity of reasoning; it needs grace to escape from the distortions of pride and acquisitiveness.

The ecological crisis challenges us to be reasonable. Put like that, it sounds banal. But given the level of *irrationality* around the question, it is well worth saying, especially if we are clear about the roots of reasoning in these "skills" of negotiating the world of material objects.

I don't intend to discuss in detail the rhetoric of those who deny the reality of climate change, except to say that rhetoric (as King Canute demonstrated) does not turn back rising waters.

If you live in Bangladesh or Tuvalu, scepticism about global warming is precisely the opposite of reasonable: "negotiating" this environment means recognising the fact of rising sea levels; and understanding what is happening necessarily involves recognising how rising temperatures affect sea levels.

It is possible to argue about the exact degree to which human intervention is responsible for these phenomena (though it would be a quite remarkable coincidence if massively increased levels of carbon emissions merely happened to accompany a routine cyclical change in global temperatures, given the obvious explanatory force of the presence of these emissions), but it is not possible rationally to deny what the inhabitants of low-lying territories in the world routinely face as the most imminent threat to their lives and livelihoods.

And what the perspective of faith – in particular of Christian faith – brings to this discussion is the insight that we are not and don't have to be God. For us to be reasonable and free and responsible is for us to live in awareness of our *limits and dependence.* It is no lessening of our dignity as humans, let alone our rationality and liberty as humans, if we exercise these "godlike" gifts in the context of bodies that are fragile and mortal and a world that we do not completely control.

What might an intelligent response to the environmental crisis look like?

Let us look at our carefully defined common values and in the renewal of our living through the articulating and promoting of such values – including the recognition of the interdependence of all things and of the equal significance of diverse kinds of "capital" – social and human as much as material or natural.

In other words, intelligence comes to life when a kind of empathy and imagination is stirred by a new vision of things: intelligence alone does not generate new vision, and bare argument does not on the whole change things; but vision displayed in new forms of human life and engagement can renew intelligence in the sense I have been giving to the word. And this is where the significance of the perspectives of faith is most obvious.

Renewing the face of the earth, then, is an enterprise not of imposing some private human vision on a passive nature but of living in such a way as to bring more clearly into light the deep interconnectedness of all things and their dependence on what we cannot finally master or understand.

This involves a creative engagement with nature, seeking to work with those natural powers whose working gives us joy, as St Augustine says, in order to enhance human liberty and well-being. But that creative work will always be done in consciousness of costs, seen and unseen, and will not be dominated by fantasies about unconditional domination. It is a vision that, in the Christian context, is founded on the idea of humanity as having a "priestly" relationship with the natural order: the human agent is created with the capacity to make sense of the environment and to move it into a closer relation with its creator by drawing out of it its capacity to become a sign of love and generosity.

This entails so using the things of the earth that they promote justice between human beings – making sense so as to make peace, equity and so on, using the skills of negotiating the environment in order to alleviate suffering and spread resources. Used in this way, the raw material of the environment is seen as serving human need – but only by being used in awareness of its own integrity and its own constraints. It remains itself, but in its use for the sake of healing or justice becomes "sacramental" of the infinite gift from which it originates.

The "face" of the earth becomes an aspect of the face of God.
So this is why Christians are bound to set all this discussion in the context of that divine practice which decisively redeems humankind. God relationship with himself through the life, death and resurrection of Jesus: he shows his face to us and – as St Paul says in the second letter he wrote to Christians in Corinth – our own faces are "unveiled" as we advance towards God.
We are revealed for who or what we are. And in this event we become able to reveal what the entire material world is for, to display it as a sign of love by our loving and just use of it – and by our contemplative respect for it and our capacity to let it be: in a way a re-creation of our intelligence.
Technology, some have pointed out, is toxic when it forgets the artistic and transformational dimension – that is (in the terms I've been using here) when it loses its proper human intelligence. One particular image that perhaps expresses

most simply what a Christian account of responsibility in our environment comes down to.

In his book *Variations on the Song of Songs*, Christos Yannaros speaks of how love compels you to see things differently – to love "the landscapes we have looked at together."

And so if we fall in love with God, even fleetingly, all the sense impressions of this world become part of such a common "landscape". I begin to see it with his eyes and so to sense in it the promise of his beauty.

Now it may be a long way from the technicalities of recalculating economic gains in terms of environmental cost to the experience of what has been called "erotic joy" in relation to God. But the distinctive Christian approach to responsibility for our environment has somehow to hold these two languages together.

Finally, our care for the world we inhabit is not simply a duty laid upon us but a dimension of life made whole: a redeeming activity grounded in the character of our own redemption, a revelation of the true "face" of creation as we ourselves undergo the uncovering of our own human face before God.

Going back to the root meaning of the Hebrew word, what we're asked to undertake is in fact a conversion – a turning – towards the truth: towards the God who is eternally active and giving in ways beyond our concepts, towards the hidden depths of who we ourselves are – and thus towards the face of the earth, seeing it freshly in its unfathomable interrelatedness.

As Psalm 104 in the Old Testament has it, when God hides his face, creation is locked in fear and slips towards death; when he breathes on creation (when he "sends his spirit"), creation happens all over again, and the face of the earth is renewed. That turning of the Spirit towards the movement that carries our love and intelligence in the same direction, so that we can properly make answer for, be responsible for, our world.

So the environment, and, part of it, climate change, are undoubtedly among my central concerns. This is without doubt a *moral* issue and a subject I have frequently been drawn to speak on.

Here for example are some of my thoughts as expressed at a meeting with members of the Tyndall Centre for Climate Change Research in London in 2006.

The fundamental question is surely *who we are, where do we belong?* Do we belong anywhere in this world? Because it seems that we behave as if we didn't.

One of the underlying moral and imaginative questions that arises in thinking about climate change and the wider environmental agenda is this habit, this ingrained tradition, of behaving as if we didn't belong, as if we were not part of an interactive system, as if we were brains on stalks.

So the moral question is not simply, as we often hear, about what we *do*. It is about imagining who we are, reviving that sense of being part of a system, not one that imprisons or crushes us, but one in which we become who we are by interaction. It's as true of our place overall, as it is true of our social destiny, and possibility, as social and political beings. But to begin there, is of course to remind ourselves that we're now more and more in a world in which conventional political patterns, and conventional ideas of local and national sovereignties, are challenged in all sorts of ways by the number of problems we face that cannot be addressed or resolved by one nation, one jurisdiction, alone.

The challenges the environmental crisis poses are challenges which need to be addressed by global citizenship, that's to say, by a lively and practical sense of belonging to something more than just the voting community in any one locality. There are other problems like that and I would, in brackets, put in the severe problems we face here, and the far more severe problems that are faced, say in Africa, by the spread of HIV and AIDS, by the health crises that affect us and which are not wholly unconnected, of course, with the issues we're here to think about today. But, whatever the truth of that, the point is that we are now in an environment in which local resolution, local decision has to open out into global perspective.

The moral dimension comes, of course, in a sense, not only in our responsibility to people at a distance from us here and now in our world, it comes in respect to our responsibility to the future. And that's perhaps a slightly odd thing to say in some ways, but if, in justice, one sector of a public or a community is using, draining, resources at the expense of others, then if we have a longer view than just the contemporary, what we are currently involved in is a fantastically and manifestly unjust situation where those who happen to be alive at the moment are draining off the resource from that vast future community who need to live in a habitable and a just world.

The interaction here of ecology and economy becomes crucial in the present, and in respect to the future. So that another dimension of our moral imagination here, has to be a stronger and stronger sense of what we owe to the future. You can talk about that in terms that sound a bit woolly and aspirational, but the fact is that we behave, most of the time, as if we trusted that there would be a human future. We beget children, we leave legacies, we make records, but how are we actively going to continue to make a sustainable, habitable environment? That, I suggest, is a question of justice.

So justice is very clearly part of what we address, and part of what excites me about the research project on climate change is the way in which a whole range of disciplines, areas of research and resource, are being held together. We're encouraged not to forget the connections between ecology and economy; we're being encouraged to see that issues about development cannot be counter-poised to issues about environmental justice, and we're being encouraged quite simply, to be exact and precise about the knowledge we need in order to address the crisis.

We need to think about this in relation to those questions of the unequal balance of power in our world between wealthy and poor, and I'm very excited to see the way in which those themes are woven so consistently into the programmes of the years ahead of the Tyndall project.

And of course all of this would be completely empty if we were not, at the same time, talking about the empowering of ordinary agents here in the United Kingdom, agents like you and me. When we're confronted with these problems that require global consciousness, global citizenship, it's very easy to think that this is much too big, this is something where I'm incapable of making a difference.

Those of you who share my enthusiasm for *The Simpsons* television programmes may remember that wonderful episode where Homer runs for public office on the slogan

"Can't someone else do it?"

And wins!

As he probably would in many electoral contexts, but I'll say no more about that for now.

And so, all of this ought to issue in a much stronger sense for the ordinary citizen here of what's possible; what's *do-able*. The exactitude of the research, the breadth of the scope of the research, is not something that ought to distract us from these very basic and practical questions.

So I hope that the fruit of research will be not only that high level professional resourcing of our public and intellectual discourse about this, but also the sense of empowerment for the ordinary citizen, and perhaps even the ordinary church.

I know that it's customary, in some people's eyes, for the Church to make large moral statements about things that it doesn't really do very much about and, before that is said, I hope that we can really address this in our own context, speaking as a member of the Church of England. And we are about to launch precisely that project within our Church, a

'Shrinking the Footprint' exercise which will ask every church, every diocesan office, every national institution of the Church of England, to measure its energy consumption, and begin to set targets. It's a small beginning, but at the moment we haven't got that information; we need to have it, and that kind of auditing activity is of course one of the places to start for any individual, any household, and any organisation.

So, in the work that lies ahead, in the change of awareness that we all of us here desperately hope to see, I hope I can say that the Church of England is fully behind this effort and involved in this effort. And I know that you will tell us if we're falling behind, and not let us forget; and I challenge those present to keep us up to the mark on that. We have a number of tasks to go forward with here, but if we and other public institutions can clearly set some standards, both for auditing and for target setting, (or rather more importantly, for target meeting - a sensitive point), then we shall be spreading a little bit of good news around. I come at this question, obviously, as somebody who believes that we're here because we are meant to be here in the purposes of God, but for me being 'meant to be here in the purposes of God', means meant to be here in the material, vulnerable, interactive world which I have to respect as deeply and seriously as I have to respect other parts of the human creation. That's the challenge which Christians and other religious persons have to internalise and rise to, but it's a challenge which really makes claims on all of our capacity to extend our hearts and minds to envision ourselves afresh; as I said at the beginning, to develop a new, more rooted, more serious, sense of who we are and where we truly belong.

9

Finishing (for now)

Obviously it's always presumptuous to sign off a letter to someone you don't know by saying 'with love'. But in so far as I long for the person I'm writing to flourish and be themselves and be joyful, I hope I *can* say 'love'.

So I hope I can say to Lulu, and to you, 'with love'.

So -

"I think God would end by sending lots of love."

I do too

Rowan

If you liked this...

- You might also enjoy

Paula Clifford, Angels with Trumpets. The Church in a Time of Global Warming, Darton Longman and Todd, 2009
C S Lewis, The lion, the witch and the wardrobe, Macmillan, 1950
Robert Murray, The cosmic covenant, Sheed & Ward, 1992
Rowan Williams, Being Human: bodies, minds, persons, SPCK. Publishing, 2018.

References and Acknowledgements

References for works mentioned in the text

Internet links

- (https://www.bbc.co.uk/news/entertainment-arts-43547436/) [Justin Bieber]

- https://anglicanalliance.org/ [Anglican Alliance]

- https://www.amazon.co.uk/Lion-Witch-Wardrobe-Chronicles-Narnia/dp/0007323123 [Narnia books]

- https://www.bbc.co.uk/programmes/p00947fc/ [Desert Island Discs]
- http://aoc2013.brix.fatbeehive.com/articles.php/1759/climate-change-a-moral-issue-address-to-the-tyndall-centre/ [transcript of lecture on climate change, Tyndall, Centre]

- https://www.theguardian.com/commentisfree/belief/2009/mar/26/religion-anglicanism/ [text of 2009 Ebor lecture]

- http://aoc2013.brix.fatbeehive.com/articles.php/1752/rowan-williams-on-poetry [Rowan Williams on poetry at the Guy's and St Thomas' Hospital NHS Trust Annual Arts Event, 2009]

Books and lectures etc. referred to

- William Blake, Collected Poems (any edition, or any n web)

- A S Byatt, The Biographer's Tale, Chatto and Windus, 2009
- Alighieri Dante, Paradise (The Divine Comedy, Part 3), translated by Dorothy Sayers, Penguin, 1962

- T S Eliot, Collected poems, Faber

- John Keats, Collected Poems (any edition, or on web)

- C S Lewis, Chronicles of Narnia, HarperCollIns, 1950-

- C S Lewis, A Grief Observed, Faber, 1966

- Steven Mithen, The Singing Neanderthals: The Origins of Music, Language, Mind and Body, W&N, 2006

- Martin Rees, Our Final Century, Arrow, 2003
- William Shakespeare, Sonnets (any edition, or on web)
- Rowan Williams, Headwaters. Poems, Perpetua Press, 2008
- Rowan Williams, 'Our duty to the earth', Ebor Lecture, The Guardian, 26 March 2009

Acknowledgements

My thanks to those organisations where earlier versions of some of this material has appeared, in particular The Guardian Newspaper, and of course to Lulu for getting this going in the first place - and to you for perhaps hammering on about the same question...

The publishers would like to express their gratitude to the most generous photographers in the world, those of 'Unsplash' (https://unsplash.com/) for the free images reproduced here.

Questions for discussion, reflection, and action

"Dear Lulu", a letter

What do you think of this attempt to answer Lulu's good question? Convincing?

Beginning and continuing

What started you off on your current interests and commitments? And your parents or other loved ones? (You could try asking then)

Poems, poetry and how they happen

Do you yourself find that reading (or writing) poetry helps you to better get a grip on things... explore stillness in some way? (Perhaps you find visual images or music or sport do it better for you, if so perhaps worth thinking about that)?

"...explore and celebrate what is and *what might be..."* all very well to *say* that, but think about it: is it something that you too like to do? If so how? In poetry? In other ways (science? painting? reading?). You might find it interesting to compare thoughts on this with your friends.

What do you or your friends think "might be"?

Poems can come, it seems, in several ways - are any of these true for you (or other poets or writers you know about)? Do you think it might apply to other artistic or scientific or sporting skills too? How a *sudden* scientific inspiration *('eureka!!)* perhaps coming, as they say some do, in a dream, as against a conclusion that has been long pondered and left to simmer in the unconscious till ready; or *suddenly* finding that you've mastered a particular move in football or tennis as against a slowly fermenting skill?

If you are interested in music you might like to listen to my choices in Desert Island discs and the reasons behind them

(https://www.bbc.co.uk/programmes/p00947fc/). Did you like them?
What do they and the reasoning behind them tell you about me and other Desert Island speakers? You never know, *you* might be invited someday, if so what would you choose (most likely not the same) and, equally or maybe even more important, *why* (I am sure you can make a good case for yourself: music goes very deep
Do you think there is anything in common between the way that music and poems happen? If so how?

Thinking, thoughts and Narnia

Is there really a difference, as suggested in this chapter, between 'individuals' and 'persons'? If so does it matter, and which is your best friend? Which is it better to be (not a bad question for a lively debate... which side wins and do you agree?)
Have you read any of the Narnia books? If so do you find them rather (how?) sexist? Irrelevant for your own life? Conveying

something of the same as suggested here? Do you know other books that perhaps do something of the same thing? Can fiction be a better way to convey deep truths than philosophy or theology textbooks? (You could set up a debate with people taking different sides - who wins?)

A Prison Visit

If you were in charge, what kind of prison system would you create? Why?
Are murderers people? Does it matter? (That too could and maybe should be debated)

Facing reality...

What awkward questions do *you ask?* And your friends? Does anyone answer you and if so how and does that satisfy you? And what, if asked, might *your* answer be?
If you could ask God a question directly (about anything), what would it be? What would your best friend's be? Try drafting a letter in response to either question, then

share and discuss it. Do you think from trying this, that it was hard to write that letter, if so why?

Our precious world - thoughts on environment and climate

What are your own views on all this? And your friends' and teachers' and so on?
What difference to the climate and environment might your own views and actions make?
How does the idea of 'our precious world' relate to what God supposedly says to Lulu about ways that people 'discover' him? And would the same be true of you or your loved ones (you could ask ...)?

Finishing (for now)

If you were asked what you'd got out of this book, what would you reply?
Now that you have had a chance to think further about it, what do you think about "God's" letter to Lulu?
Given the chance would *you* have written it differently? (Well you do have the chance - you don't have to be an

archbishop to share your ideas with people out there in the Hearing Others' Voices Facebook page)?
Your opinion is as good as anyone else's - and you don't have to impress anyone, remember?
Given the chance would *you* have written it differently? (Well you do have the chance, bits if it anyway - you don't have to be an archbishop to share your ideas with people out there in the Hearing Others' Voices Facebook page? Your opinion is as good as anyone else's after all!)
How, in short, would you have replied to Lulu?

References

Did you look at any of these? If so why, and were they as you expected and did you like them? (Or not - up to you of course. Are any in your local or school (etc.) library? (You could always suggest one or two if you think others might like them)

The Hearing Others' Voices Facebook community

Welcome from us all, specially the HOV series editors Ruth and Roh!
https://m.facebook.com/HearingOthers?_rdr
We all look forward to your ideas and questions and arguments and (seriously!) criticisms and challenges.

Hearing Others' Voices

Photos and videos too, and links to lots of music please, your own and others' - the series is 'Hearing Others' Voices', so that's what it's all about.

Lightning Source UK Ltd.
Milton Keynes UK
UKHW030635140121
377037UK00010B/1237